MILITARY HELICOPTERS

Modern Military Techniques

MODERN MILITARY TECHNIQUES
MILITARY HELICOPTERS

James D. Ladd

Illustrations by
Peter Sarson & Tony Bryan

Lerner Publications Company • Minneapolis

Library of Congress Cataloging-in-Publication Data

Ladd, James D.
  Military helicopters.

  (Modern military techniques)
  Includes index.
  Summary: Describes how helicopters perform compli-
cated military maneuvers and includes detailed illustra-
tions explaining their weapons and control systems.
    1. Military helicopters—Juvenile literature.
[1. Military helicopters. 2. Helicopters] I. Sarson,
Peter, ill. II. Title. III. Series.
UG1230.L34   1987   623.74′6047   86-10693
ISBN 0-8225-1382-X (lib. bdg.)

Manufactured in the United States of America

    4   5   6   7   8   9   10   95   94   93   92   91   90   89

CONTENTS

1 The History of Military Helicopters

The first military helicopters to fly with the American Air Commando in 1944 during its operations in Burma were experimental machines. But the following year the Sikorsky R-4s came into service with the American army for reconnaissance. They had been developed by Ivan Sikorsky's company. He had flown the first VS-300 with its powered rotors on September 14, 1939, when he proved that not only did these lift it off the ground, but that the tail rotor prevented the helicopter from spinning in reaction to the main rotor's power-to-rotate (torque).

The military uses for helicopters were soon apparent, but the early machines could easily be damaged by rifle fire. They vibrated to make any

steady aiming of their weapons almost impossible and could not lift any worthwhile load. Yet within a generation, Sikorsky had overcome these difficulties and built practical military aircraft that might hover, could lift more than their two-man crew and were reliable.

Another early manufacturer was the Bell Helicopter Company who built a few 200-hp machines for the American army to fly in Korea in the early 1950s. But this small aircraft could lift little more than its pilot and copilot. In June 1955 the company began building a more powerful machine, the Iroquois HU-1A, nicknamed the "Huey." It had a 700-hp engine that could use a

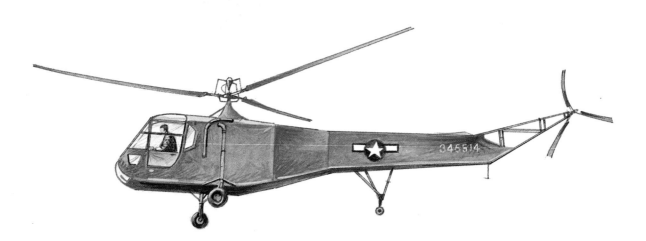

variety of fuels and gave much more power for its weight than previous engines.

In the 1960s and '70s the war in Vietnam led to major developments in military helicopters and in their weapons. The "Huey" — redesignated the UH-1 in 1962 — was modified, the power of its engine increased and the fuselage enlarged to provide a cabin which would carry twelve soldiers. These UH-1Ds flew American troops to react quickly to enemy raids in Vietnam, to set up ambushes, evacuate casualties and carry out many tasks, some of which had previously been jobs for Jeeps.

Early in this period of development the Bell Company tested the UH-1B which had a pair of auxiliary jet engines to give added speed and lift. This became in 1962 the first of the anti-tank attack helicopters, the AH-1G Cobra. Over 1,100 had been built by 1971, and all manner of weapons might be fired by its observer-gunner. He sat in the nose of the plane with the pilot sitting above and behind him in tandem. The gunner might fire twin-machine guns or six-barreled miniguns from a turret under the nose. Another weapon fit was a single minigun and a grenade-launcher for use against troops in the open on the ground. The Cobra could carry 300 grenades of 40mm for this launcher. Rocket pods, 30mm cannons and later TOW missiles could be fitted to the Cobra's stub wings.

In Britain the Westland factory at Yeovil in Somerset had been building seaplanes for the Royal Navy since 1915 and during the Second World War built the Lysander high-winged monoplane for reconnaissance. After that war this factory, by then the Westland Company, built the Dragonfly in 1950, a version of the Sikorsky S-51 light helicopter. In the following thirty years Westland became one of the two largest builders of helicopters outside America, the other being the French Aerospatiale Company. In the 1980s Westland's range includes the Sea King and its Commando version, a variety of Lynx for armies and navies and the Gazelle light helicopter.

New types of helicopter are being built by Westland jointly with French and with Italian companies. Such cooperation is necessary because of the high cost of building what have become complicated machines, even if they are much easier to fly than the early helicopters.

The Modern Helicopter

There are three main types of helicopter used in modern warfare: the combat helicopter armed to attack tanks and infantry, the transport helicopter which is virtually a flying "truck", and smaller helicopters used mainly for reconnaissance and evacuating casualties. A few helicopters are equipped for special tasks such as the detection of the enemy's radio signals, his radar beams and similar electronic activity. Some are also built as flying cranes, able to lift heavy bridging structures and other equipment to places wheeled vehicles cannot reach.

The armed forces of the major powers use all these types; the Americans have over 6,000 in service. The Russians have some 2,600 combat helicopters and many more for transport. The British have 500 including those with the Royal Navy, for the "chopper" is as useful in operations at sea as it is over land.

2 The Tank Killer

Until the 1980s pilots had difficulty flying in the dark since they found it difficult to judge their position relative to the ground when flying at night. But the introduction of electronic aids to navigation and special night goggles, by which a pilot can see almost as well at night as he can in the day, has overcome this problem and enabled helicopters to be flown in the dark.

All helicopters have the obvious advantage of being able to fly quickly over country which can only be crossed slowly, if it can be crossed at all, by wheeled or tracked vehicles, although the helicopter is vulnerable to anti-aircraft fire. In battle the pilot must skim the ground along valleys, down the cleared forest lanes which are firebreaks or use other features of the countryside to prevent these gunners getting a clear shot at his aircraft. Such low flying does however enable him to surprise a tank's crew, as his helicopter suddenly appears from behind a hill or out of a forest.

Weapons on an attack helicopter such as an Apache AH-64 may include not only anti-tank missiles but — in military terms as a "weapons platform"— also air-to-air missiles, a 30mm quick-firing Chain Gun and grenade launchers for attacking infantry in the open. To attack a tank the pilot might use TOW, a tube-launched (T), optically tracked (O) and wire-guided (W) missile which is rocket propelled at over 600 mph (1,000km/h). This missile will hit the target provided

the pilot keeps it in his sights, for its track is automatically corrected by signals sent along two wires from the helicopter as these stream out behind the missile. He can aim his missile a distance of 2.25 miles (3.75 km) but as the target has to be in clear view, the effective range is much shorter at perhaps 3,300 feet (1,000m) especially in hilly country which can hide a tank as well as a helicopter.

There is — as you will see in later sections — much more for the pilot to do than simply aim his TOW missile, but once this hits a tank, the high explosive armor-piercing warhead will destroy it. TOW missiles can also destroy enemy bunkers or other strong points in his defense lines, targets which are attacked by helicopters supporting the advance of rapidly moving columns with infantry in armored personnel carriers. At one time this could only be done by the artillery, but they had difficulty in keeping self-propelled guns supplied with ammunition when a column moved quickly, whereas the helicopter can fly back to a forward

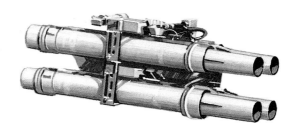

A pod of four tubes for TOW missiles mounted on a Lynx AH1. Each is fired by a rocket motor that burns out. Small wings and tail fins spring open as a second motor fires to sustain the missile's flight, which is guided by movement of the fins.

base to rearm after launching a series of attacks. It therefore has become not only a tank destroyer but also in part replaced artillery in the support of advancing columns.

3
Anti-Tank Tactics

A flight of three or four helicopters can surprise enemy tanks 12 miles (20km) or more behind the main battle where tank crews, not expecting to be attacked, are vulnerable with their hatch covers open. Helicopters may patrol valleys in enemy territory looking for such targets, but they are more likely to lie in wait behind a hill (see below) ready to ambush tanks spotted by a Forward Air Controller

(FAC) who with his radio operator has already infiltrated into enemy territory, protected by a patrol from Special Forces such as the SAS or the American Rangers.

The position of the targets given by the FAC cannot be seen by the pilots because they are flying so close to the valley floor that — like the nap of cloth — they are almost on the ground. This method of flying is known as "nap of earth" (NOE) style. However once the pilots have reached the designated target they must be able to fire their missiles and fly clear of the valley quickly because their action is likely to alert enemy anti-aircraft gunners or missile crews stationed in rear areas.

If the pilot uses TOW he would have to guide the missile to the target. Therefore he uses Hellfire — "helliborne-launched fire-and-forget" — missiles, or similar types. He need only fire these in the general direction of the target because the FAC will guide them on the final part of their flight.

This is done with a beam of laser light, its light impulses being emitted in a code which the missile's

FAC

sensors seek and then follow. Indeed if there are several beams with different codes, then several missiles can have sensors set so that each one picks up a different beam, even though they are fired from the helicopters within fractions of a second of each other. More usually the FAC has a single beam, aiming this at the leading tank of a group to guide in the first Hellfire. As this explodes he swings his beam onto the second tank and the second missile finds the beam, follows it and hits the second tank.

Meanwhile the helicopters fly clear of the ambush position, keeping low because this gives the enemy's radar less opportunity to lock onto the aircraft before these are into the next valley.

Should the enemy aim anti-aircraft missiles or shells at the retreating planes, these may track a helicopter by several means. They may seek the infrared light in the heatwaves from its exhaust, they may have sensors that home in on the aircraft's radar or they may be guided by radio signals from the launching crew. The pilot can protect his helicopter against these attacks. His plane is designed to make infrared sensors less likely to find the engine's exhaust because it is cooled. Special flares with an intense heat can be fired to attract the infrared sensors of some missiles away. Signals from an electronic device may be sent out to confuse the sensors trying to follow his radar beams back to the plane. This device can also be used to jam signals from the ground which are guiding a missile. The pilot can also drop chaff to confuse radar sets which are trying to track him.

With luck and good flying the helicopter pilot will keep clear of defenses, returning over friendly forces. Their radar picks up a special signal that identifies his aircraft as being friendly by an electronic device, the Indentifier of Friend from Foe (IFF), which is carried in all military aircraft. The whole operation might take 90 minutes. The pilot would normally only be expected to fly five such missions a day because they require great concentration by him and his crew if they are not to make a careless mistake and be shot down.

Laser beam to tanks

Flight path of missile

4 Combat Helicopter Battalions

Pilots and crews are expected to fly for only a limited time each day. Such limits might be exceeded in an emergency, but their helicopters cannot be flown without taking dangerous risks if these have not been properly serviced, a job that even a skilled team of mechanics and fitters need several hours to complete with the thoroughness required to be sure not only the engines and airframe are sound, but also all the equipment aboard is in full working order. Therefore all military helicopter units have more ground staff than fliers but organize units in different ways.

The British have squadrons of transport helicopters with the RAF and combat helicopters manned by the Army Air Corps. Up to five of the Air Corps' regiments are in Germany at any one time, each with a squadron of Lynx with TOW missiles and a squadron of Gazelle AH 1 reconnaissance helicopters. The regiment is under the overall command of the armored division in which it is serving, but the Corps commander may reallocate squadrons to other divisions for particular missions.

The Americans have Air Cavalry Attack Brigades with mechanized infantry divisions as well as other types of helicopter units. An Attack Brigade (see chart) has 42 attack helicopters (AHs) and 130 general purpose utility helicopters (UHs) used for recces, mine laying, transporting senior officers across a battlefield, evacuating casualties, and as flying command posts. Information on the progress of the battle may be provided from obser-

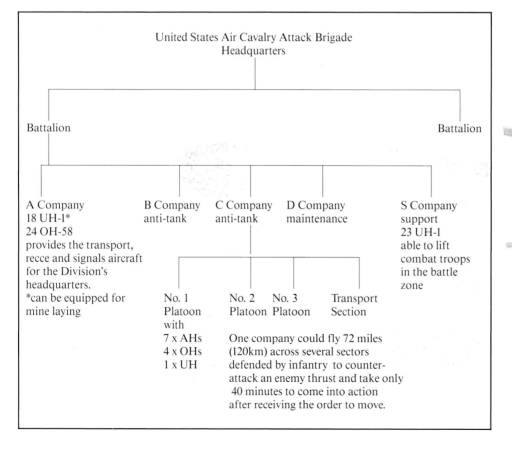

United States Air Cavalry Attack Brigade
Headquarters

Battalion

Battalion

A Company
18 UH-1*
24 OH-58
provides the transport, recce and signals aircraft for the Division's headquarters.
*can be equipped for mine laying

B Company
anti-tank

C Company
anti-tank

D Company
maintenance

S Company
support
23 UH-1
able to lift combat troops in the battle zone

No. 1 Platoon with
7 x AHs
4 x OHs
1 x UH

No. 2 Platoon

No. 3 Platoon

Transport Section

One company could fly 72 miles (120km) across several sectors defended by infantry to counter-attack an enemy thrust and take only 40 minutes to come into action after receiving the order to move.

vation helicopters (OHs) equipped for reconnaissance. These may also spot targets.

Each company has twelve OHs, some of which work with its twenty-one attack copters — AH-1S Cobras or the more modern AH-64 Apaches. The company's three UHs provide transport to carry forward urgently needed ammunition, to evacuate casualties and fulfil many other tasks requiring rapid transport while the transport section sets up forward refueling points with small teams of technicians for emergency servicing.

Other Western nations have similar companies, those in the German army being equipped with 28 *Panzerabwehr-Hubschauber* (PAH-1) in four platoons of seven aircraft. These companies do not have their own wheeled vehicles but rely on other sub-units of the battle group to provide these. In battle all helicopter companies work closely with the infantry who radio information on targets, but the German pilots of PAH-1s work in particularly close radio contact as they have no scout or observation helicopters (OHs) in their companies. The German OH companies, each with ten heli-

copters, are independently under the command of a division's staff, with an OH company in each division.

The Russians have a different organization as their helicopters, mainly flown by air force pilots, are under the command of the general commanding a field army. This higher level of command helps to ensure that the three squadrons in the regiment with each army are used to the best advantage, since the Russians have relatively few combat helicopters. Each squadron has twenty aircraft, two with *Hind* Ds or Es and one with Mi-8 Es that can carry a dozen soldiers as well as four anti-tank missiles and 192 smaller rockets. Such a squadron might be attached to a battle group for an operation to be completed in a week or two, after which the squadron returns to its field army command.

The Russian Mi-24 *Hind* D cruises at 90 mph (150 km/h) and can reach 180 mph (300 km/h) briefly when making an attack — its "dash" speed. Armed with four 12.7mm machine guns under its nose, 80 or more rockets and four anti-tank missiles, it is a large and formidable helicopter, able to withstand damage as its stub wings add to the rotor's lift.

5
The Anatomy of a Helicopter

1 Nose window
2 Air grill
3 Radio in nose and electronics bay
4 Windshield wipers
5 Windshield panels
6 Rudder pedals
7 Window for pilot to see downwards
8 Control column
9 Cockpit door
10 Boarding step
11 Sliding window
12 Copilot's seat
13 Axle fairing with step to cockpit
14 Port navigation light
15 Handrail containing aerials

16 Gunner's sliding window (open)
17 Cooling grill
18 Main undercarriage
19 M-23D 7.62mm machine gun (port side)

20 Undercarriage shock absorbers
21 Side-facing gunner's seat
22 Cargo hook loads for up to 7,986 (3,630 kg) slung beneath the helicopter

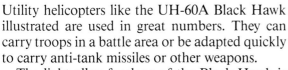

Utility helicopters like the UH-60A Black Hawk illustrated are used in great numbers. They can carry troops in a battle area or be adapted quickly to carry anti-tank missiles or other weapons.

The light alloy fuselage of the Black Hawk is specially built to give protection around the cabin. This and other safety features help to prevent injuries to the three-man crew and their eleven passengers should the UH-60 crash land. Other features of its design make it compact enough to be loaded in a US Air Force C-141 Starlift or other types of large transports so that it may be carried across continents to reach a threatened area.

Dimensions:

Main rotor diameter	16.36m
Overall length with rotors turning	19.76m
Height	3.76m
Weight when loaded for mission	7,375kg
Maximum cruising speed at 1,220m	269km/h

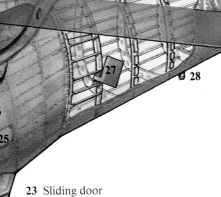

23 Sliding door
24 Spring-loaded step for maintenance
25 Connection to take fuel pressurized for quick refueling
26 Fuel tanks (one of two each holding 154.44 gallons (594 liters)
27 Chaff dispenser
28 Anti-collision light
29 Tail wheel assembly
30 Folding footrest
31 Pivot for tail plane
32 Hydraulic jack to move tailplane
33 Aerial for the radio of the cargo troops' commander
34 Anti-collision light
35 Graphite epoxy composite rotor blades

36 Tail rotor drive gearbox
37 Pitch change spider
38 Tail rotor which is canted at 20°
39 Leading edge of fin with suppressed aerial
40 Tail planes
41 Formation lights
42 Communications aerial
43 Tail cone frame
44 Transmission shaft to tail rotor
45 Engine exhaust pipe
46 Auxiliary power unit and exhaust
47 Seats for troops or area for cargo
48 Fire extinguisher
49 Exhaust cooling fan to reduce heat and therefore infrared light waves
50 Cabin floor
51 Port engine of two T700-GE-700 turboshaft engines
52 Oil cooler exhaust designed for infrared suppression
53 Oil cooler fan
54 Folding step for maintenance

55 Gear boxes
56 Blade pitch control rods
57 Fixed trailing edge tabs
58 Main blades of fiberglass on a titanium spar
59 Leading edge drooped
60 Main rotor head in which blades of rotor are adjustable, to give different angles (the pitch) at which they strike the air
61 Rotor mast
62 Air intake for starboard engine
63 Sliding cover over equipment
64 Cabin heater
65 External stores support system (each side)
66 Airspeed indicator pitot tubes
67 Electric fuses
68 Armored headrest
69 Cockpit "eyebrow" windows
70 Armored seat backs
71 Central instrument console
72 Pilot's seat
73 Sliding panel of side armor

15

6 Weapon Systems

The weapons carried may be varied to suit particular missions. But their weight, including the weight of any electronic equipment to guide them, any extra fuel or cargo and additional armor plate to protect the crew, limits what may be carried. The Black Hawk might carry an M56 mine dispenser that when dropped spreads anti-personnel mines over an area of ground. If the area to be mined is far behind enemy lines, extra fuel tanks would be needed to increase the normal 100 minutes the Hawk can be airborne to five hours. Flight times are calculated to allow the helicopter to cruise for most of this time but fly at over 180 miles per hour (300km/h) for part of it. The weight of the fuel needed for the flight would necessitate a lighter load of weapons.

Helicopters can also be affected by the air's temperature. The hot air of the tropics can be less resistant to the rotors, making them less able to lift the weight they can usually manage.

In normal conditions, the AH-64 Apache (opposite) may carry the following missiles for attacking both aircraft and tanks as well as weapons for attacking troops on the ground:

A. *AIM-9P Sidewinder air-to-air missiles*
These are powered by a solid-fuel rocket and have sensors which home in on the infrared (IR) heat waves from an enemy plane, or they may have an optical guidance system which sights the target and tracks it. Each weighs 189.2 pounds (86kg) and has a high explosive warhead that bursts its casing in a deadly ring of fragments.

B. *2.75-inch (70mm) rockets*
Carried in pods of nineteen from which a selected number may be fired in salvos, these are not guided but aimed at troops or unarmored ("soft") vehicles and other targets which may be damaged by their explosive warheads.

C. *Hellfire missiles*
Each weighs 94.6 pounds (43kg) and the latest designs have rocket motors which give off little or no telltale smoke, which could guide the enemy back to the helicopter that launched it. They may be fitted with sensors that home in on the radar guiding enemy air defenses making them an Air Defense Suppression Missile (ADSM). The electronics in the aircraft to launch Hellfire weighs only 59.4 pounds (27kg), against 446.6 pounds (203kg) for TOW's aiming devices and sights.

D. *M230 Hughes Chain Gun*
This fires 750 rounds in a minute. These may be high-explosive, armor-piercing or other cannon shells, which when fired in bursts have a cumulative effect far greater than would be expected from the damage caused by single rounds.

E. *Radar and other sensors*
The helicopter crew use these to aim their various weapons. Shown here in the nose of the aircraft, a position that has some limitations. Masthead sights have been developed for mounting above the rotors so they can protrude above the tree tops, while the aircraft hovers with its fuselage hidden from view and from a clear shot by machine-gunners or anti-aircraft guns.

In the masthead sight (right) designed by the staff of McDonnell Douglas are: a television camera that gives the pilot a view over the trees, a laser beam that may be used as a rangefinder or set up in a different way to guide missiles like Hellfire, a thermal imager which sees a picture in the infrared of heat waves, and the equivalent of an open sight known as the "bore sight." This last sight has to be specially set in such a way that the aiming line from

D   **Hughes chain gun**

it to the target will point the barrel of say the Chain Gun at the target correctly, even though the gun is perhaps about 13 feet (4m) below the sight.

All the information from this 26-inch (65cm) sphere is fed down a tube of only .88 inch (22mm) to displays in the cockpit. The pilot's controls for moving the sphere left or right and tilting it are fed back up the same tube! These controls may also set the laser or other sensor to track a target. The helicopter's computer processes the information and even if a target moves behind trees or other cover, the equipment predicts where it will reappear.

The crew may correctly align any of the three sensors — TV, laser or thermal imager — with the bore sight in 30 seconds. While any of these or the radar in the nose may take six seconds to lock onto a target, it takes longer to aim the weapons. Nevertheless the pilot may set switches to fire several of these weapons while the copilot aims a TOW missile. Its sight automatically remains on the target even though the helicopter is maneuvering. The onboard computer makes sure that by firing one weapon, the crew do not upset the aim of second.

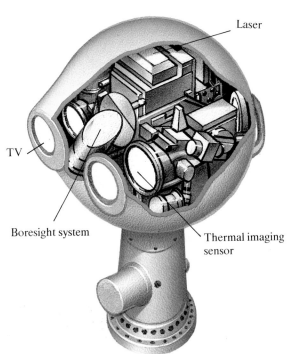

Mast head sight

17

7
The Crew and Their Instruments

The crew of most army combat helicopters consists of the pilot and copilot. In some larger aircraft there is also a gunner who fires one or other of the two heavy machine guns or quick-firing cannon on each side of the cabin.

The pilot's controls, many of which are duplicated for the copilot, can be broadly grouped in four categories: those for flying the aircraft, those for controlling its engines, those which help in navigation, and those described earlier for aiming its weapons. All the information provided by these instruments is also fed into the main computer as is other information, and this computer can then automatically co-ordinate the various systems. It also monitors what is happening, warning the pilot by a red light and audible buzzer if he has insufficient engine power for the rate of climb he intends. Such computers, known as advanced Avionic Management Systems (AMS), will enable one man to fly and fire all the weapons of a helicopter.

Flight Controls

The flight controls consist of a main control column — the cyclic. As the pilot moves this, the pitch of the main rotor blade is altered to move the helicopter forwards, backwards or to hold it hovering over one spot. In the hover the helicopter can be turned to the right or left by using the foot pedals; these alter the pitch of the tail rotor blades. Large helicopters also have tail planes which help to push the nose up or down while in flight.

On the main column in some helicopters are switches to control various items of equipment which the pilot uses while flying the plane, such as

a mast-mounted sight if one is fitted. Also on the column is a button to fire the weapons which he has selected by setting different switches.

The Console

The instruments and switches are set out so that the ones used most frequently are the easiest to read or reach. In the illustration, display 1 shows the position of the aircraft relative to the horizontal. Display 2 shows how far it has turned left or right of the intended course. Indicators 4, 5 and 6 give the settings and state of the automatic pilot, by which the computer flies the helicopter. Display 7 tells the copilot how high the aircraft is above sea level.

Some displays — like those at 9 — may be used for several different sets of information. Each being called to view by appropriate switches, as there are different sets of information provided by the computer. One set might consist of the temperature at the transmission shaft bearings, the oil pressure in the hydraulic system, and confirmation that fuel pumps are working at the correct pressures. Another set will provide information on electrical and other systems.

Engine Controls

The throttles (16) are the principal controls of the engines, increasing the power as they are opened. A wide range of other controls for the engines are usually operated by finger buttons or switches. But once switched on, these controls are adjusted by the computer to suit the power required in changing conditions.

Key to simplified cockpit controls:
**1 Horizontal situation indicators   2 Degree of turn indicator   3 Accurate clocks with sweep second-hands   4,5,6 Indicators associated with auto-pilot   7 Altimeter   8 Sets of warning lights   9 Display for checks on systems   10 Map display   11 Cabin ventilation switches   12 Display to show target distance and bearing or other information as selected   13 Four button switches to control fuel flows from tanks   14 Eight button switches to select weapons   15 Other switches to set functions of engines etc   16 Throttles.
A   First pilot's control column. B   Second pilot's control coloumn with firing button for weapon selected**

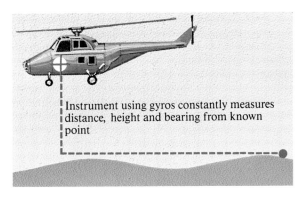

Instrument using gyros constantly measures distance, height and bearing from known point

Inertial guidance system by which pilot can constantly check his position

Navigation Aids

Several different types of visual display have replaced the folded map strapped to the pilot's knee. Display 10 constantly changes to show a map of the ground the plane is flying over. This is linked to other navigation aids including the inertial guidance system that gives an exact latitude and longitude, a device based on a gyroscope or a miniature pyramid of lasers that in broad terms "remember" every movement from the fixed location for which they have been set.

There are also radar screens, positions fixed by radio signals from satellites and other aids. But the pilot must fly his helicopter instinctively so he can devote his attention to navigation, potential targets and avoiding the enemy's air defenses.

8
Air-to-Air Combat

Any future war between major powers will involve battles between helicopters. A pilot will need not only all his electronic aids but also a high degree of skill in flying his aircraft, for he will have to out-maneuver his quarry if he is to catch his enemy helicopter before it shoots him down. Although many transport and large helicopters cannot defend themselves by clever flying because they are too cumbersome.

Combat helicopters are able to survive hits from cannon shells or at least from a limited number of these. Yet new developments in aerial weapons make combat more difficult for helicopters; hyper-velocity rockets, for example, flying at 3,000 mph (5,000km/h) hit their targets with tremendous force, having covered about 2.4 miles (4km) in 3.5 seconds. They may be launched from fixed winged aircraft as well as helicopters. In such brief but violent battles the Russian *Hind* may be at a slight disadvantage because it cannot change height as quickly as an *Apache* nor hover as easily.

Some possible maneuvers are:

1. The *High Yo-Yo* in which the pilot of the pursuing aircraft, the hunter, climbs to avoid over-shooting his quarry; once he knows if his enemy is going to turn left or right, then the pursuing air-craft climbs to avoid overshooting the quarry and rolls to come into an attacking position behind it.

2. The *Horizontal Scissors* is a defensive maneuver when the hunter is, say, short of ammunition as he meets a potential quarry flying at a similar speed. The hunter increases his rate of turn until the quarry overshoots or has passed outside the hunter's turn. Then the hunter can reverse his turn to fly behind and below the quarry, coming into a "blind" spot where the quarry cannot get his weapons — or at least some of them — to bear on the hunter.

3. The *Overshoot* . . . Had the quarry turned towards the hunter when they met, coming out a mere 495 feet (150m) apart from some woods, the hunter would be forced to *overshoot*. The hunted pilot could then turn, keeping the hunter in sight as the hunted pilot rolls level; having gained height, he can force his pursuer to fly even lower.

Had they met at greater range, then the quarry might escape by initially putting his helicopter's nose down, gaining speed to make a rolling climb that will carry him above the hunter's line of flight, who then shoots under him.

Helicopters are more liable to meet a quarry by accident than by design, unless, like some Russian helicopters, they are armed with quick-firing Gatling guns and air-to-air missiles, yet are agile enough to hunt their enemy's anti-tank helicopters. Those equipped for reconnaissance avoid such combat because their job is to observe and report, which they cannot do if they tangle with an enemy.

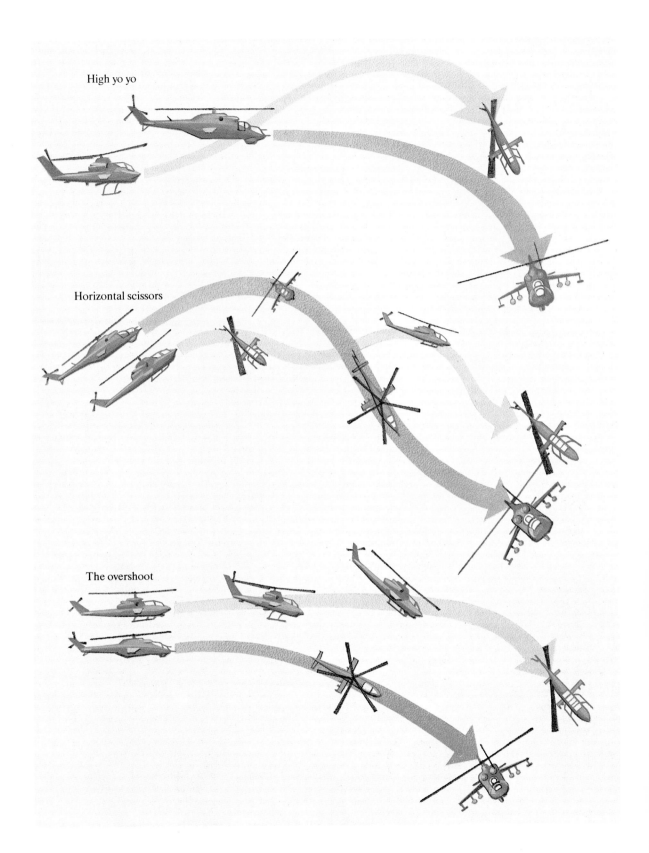

High yo yo

Horizontal scissors

The overshoot

21

9 Recce and Other Battle Helicopters

Rescue

There are times when the crew of a crashed aircraft need to be rescued before enemy ground forces can capture them. This technique was first used in Vietnam, when two heavy helicopters (HH) Sikorsky HH-3Es, known as "Jolly Green Giants," flew far into enemy territory to pick up American aircrews that had crash-landed. The HH-3Es were escorted by fighters, with an FAC in a fixed-winged aircraft to control the operation.

In the future such a rescue will be far more difficult. Therefore the Americans have developed HH-60D Night Hawks able to make lone rescue flights of 540 miles (900km), using additional fuel in tanks mounted outside the fuselage to enable them to have sufficient fuel to hover for 20 minutes over the crash, using two machine guns to counter anti-aircraft fire. Once the rescued crew have been winched aboard, they can be cared for in litters (a form of medical stretchers) during the flight home. This, like the flight out, is made close to the ground using forward looking infrared (FLIR) sensors to "read" the ground ahead. Nevertheless the pilot needs such great concentration to fly at night, when such rescues will be made, that he and the copilot will take turns in 15-minute spells.

Light helicopters are used to rescue infantry casualties, for they can dodge in behind the defenses, pick up the injured men and quickly take them to a field hospital.

Reconnaissance

The OH-58 Kiowa is a typical observation helicopter which has been in service with the American army since 1968. These aircraft are in

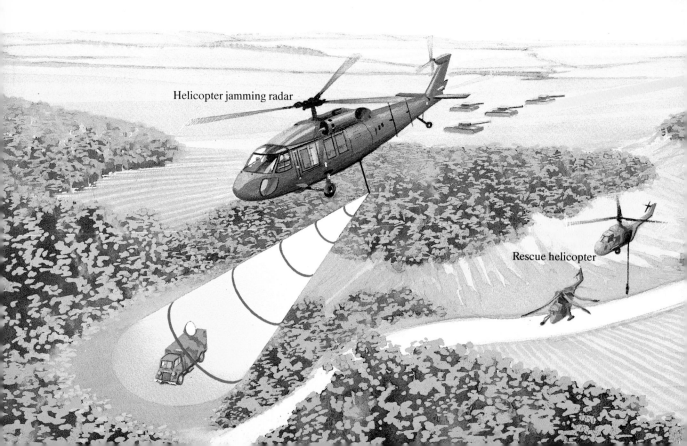

Helicopter jamming radar

Rescue helicopter

radio contact with the forward infantry companies, with attack helicopters and with a brigade or other headquarters reporting on likely targets, on the positions of friendly troops, and helping the headquarters' staff to follow the battle.

Recce helicopters may also be fitted with radar and other sensors carried in a large pod under the fuselage (see illustration). Their radar is able to indicate where enemy tanks are moving. Information from this Stand-off Target Acquisition System (SOTAS) is passed to computers on the ground that work out the point of aim for gunners in tanks.

Observation helicopter crews may use thermal imagers to detect the body heat of enemy troops hidden below trees or at night. At one time they used "sniffers" trailed below the aircraft to scent the ammonia given off by humans.

Special Electronic Mission Aircraft (SEMA)

These may be helicopters or fixed-wing aircraft with radios using a variety of aerials (antenna). Some of these eavesdrop on enemy radio messages, knowing by the volume of messages when these might be coming from a headquarters.

On the YEH-60A Quick Fix there is also a whip antennae that sends out a jamming signal, causing a high-pitched whine in the enemy's radio transmissions, drowning out the signals. Other equipment can locate radar transmissions and jam or locate the set or send signals which decoy missiles from their targets. It is even possible with some equipment to read electronically what is appearing on the visual display units (VDUs) of enemy computers, although the reader is flying at a distance above this.

Mine Laying and other Roles

Utility and other helicopters can carry underslung cages filled with mines. These have to be designed so that they will withstand being dropped when the floor of the cage is opened by remote control, yet only explode when stepped on.

A powerful searchlight may be fitted under the helicopter to light up positions where men might be hiding. The light may be infrared which can only be seen when wearing special goggles.

Recce helicopter

Mine-laying helicopter

10
The Ground Crew and Combat Maintenance

The organization of ground crews is as important as the arrangements for aircrews. Airframe fitters who repair and check the fuselage, mechanics to service the engines, armorers, instrument mechanics and those who specialize in radar, radios, or other equipment (known as "systems"), all have to work on combat and other helicopters. For major jobs, they usually work in a hangar, where rain or wind will not damage delicate circuits or cause water to seep into an hydraulic pump (many of these provide the power to move a tailplane or alter the pitch of the rotor blades).

In battle, however, there is no time between missions to make use of hangars, even if there is a suitable building nearby. The work has to be done in the open and done quickly. Teams are trained rather like racing car mechanics to check their part of the aircraft and put right any items needing repair in minutes if not seconds. Because of this speed which takes practice and familiarity with the aircraft, the crew which service a Lynx are unlikely to be able to service an AH-64 quickly.

A Lynx, for example, can land at a forward rearming and fueling point and be loaded with eight TOW missiles in three minutes while fuel is forced into its tanks under pressure to fill them in six. The pilot will keep the engines running during this "hot" refueling and is airborne again as soon as the tank is filled. If his helicopter has been damaged by enemy fire or any of his controls are not working properly, the stop will only be as long as it takes to identify the trouble and put it right. If the damage

Royal Marine Commando Air Squadron's Scout helicopters "hot" refueling in the Falkland Islands, 1982

is too great for a quick repair and the aircraft is not airworthy, then it will be lifted back by a Chinook, perhaps, to the main base.

The forward rearming point is as near the battle area as practical if not on its edge. But since only limited servicing can be done there, the helicopters fly back at the end of each series of five or six flights for proper servicing. Then the fitters and engineers strip down all those parts of the aircraft which might need some adjustment or cleaning. They top up or change the contents of reservoirs of hydraulic fluid and of oils. They test that all the controls are working smoothly. If say the change of rotor blades' pitch is jerky or stiff, fitters will find out if something is slightly bent or some coupling has worked loose. All this work takes time and is carried out against a list of jobs to be done (a check list). Some instruments need recalibrating to make sure that when they are used they give correct information. Others have to be tested to be sure that they have not been damaged in action or even "wiped" of data stored on magnetic tape. This deletion of stored programs for a computer on board might occur through an enemy's use of electronic counter-measures or through some mishap.

The maintenance at this company or flight base is limited because the technicians have only

relatively few instruments for tests, carrying only spare components that are known to need replacing frequently.

More major overhauls and repairs are carried out by the Squadron's technical staff. At their base area are a large stock of different spare parts for the airframe, engines, instruments and weapons. They also have metalworking machines, work benches and even facilities to remake a part if it is not available in the stores.

Helicopters will be flown back after they have flown for perhaps 500 hours — the number varies with different helicopters — for a major overhaul. They are then taken into the squadron's hangers

and stripped down completely in order to check and replace any damaged or worn parts. These technicians also repair parts sent back from the company's forward base as although the company may have to replace an item, it may not be damaged beyond repair but was replaced as the quickest way to keep the aircraft fit to fly.

The squadron base with its tons of spare parts, machinery and other equipment requires many heavy trucks to move it. However, various work benches, test equipment and so on may be permanently set up in a large number of container-sized "buildings" which can be moved readily with a minimum of packing.

Air engineering mechanics of the WRNS service a Wessex 5 of the Fleet Air Arm at a Royal Navy air station

11
Helicopters
Go to Sea

Flying helicopters over land is difficult enough but the pilot can usually find somewhere to put down if he has trouble. Over the sea, even if the fuselage is built to float, he can seldom put down safely far from the shore because the waves will capsize the helicopter.

Another difficulty is landing a chopper on the deck of a ship, even though the flight deck is well away from the ship's aerials and other obstructions to aircraft. The deck may be rising and falling 16 feet (about 5m) or more as the ship pitches over waves and it will be rolling from side to side if there

A Lynx on the heaving deck of a Royal Navy frigate, held securely by the snap hook of harpoon system. Right, the display panel of an Aish Ship's Motion Indicator.

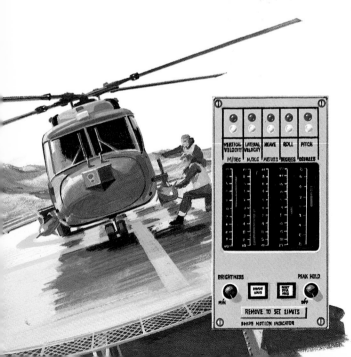

is much of a sea running. So the pilot has to judge his landing from the hover carefully or the deck may crash up into the chopper and damage its undercarriage or skids, if not something worse. The flight deck officer or a seaman help to guide the pilot in and may have an indicator which shows when the pitch and roll are too great to land safely.

Small warships have an extended wire with a clamp-hook positioned at the center of the landing spot which is marked by a painted white circle on the flight deck. As the chopper lands, a seaman snaps the hook onto a strong fixing point under the aircraft. The wire of this harpoon system is then pulled taut by a winch under the deck which then holds the helicopter firmly to the deck. On aircraft carriers several of the crew may secure each chopper, especially when the ship is moving fast. They can fold back its rotors and in some cases also fold forward the tail section, making the aircraft easier to stow in the hangar below the deck, where it is then carried on an elevator.

One of the earliest uses for naval helicopters, before they had the reliability and navigation aids of the 1980s, was — and still is — the rescue of pilots who crash into the sea while trying to land or take off. The chopper flies alongside the ship, ready to dart forward if a pilot is in the "drink," winching him to safety before his plane sinks.

In the '80s a helicopter may search for a crashed plane far from the carrier, although searching the surface of the sea needs good navigation and a well-rehearsed method. Otherwise, since it all looks the same, quite large areas will be missed by the searchers. The planes therefore fly in pre-arranged patterns which may also be used to find enemy submarines or other ships.

Some peacetime search-and-rescue (SAR) choppers are colored a bright yellow. This makes them easy to see in mist or rain or the poor visibility at dusk. In wartime the men in the water are likely to have a homing beacon. This sends out a constant radio signal which the rescuers can track to the dinghy in the water. Or they may use their thermal imagers or radar to spot the crew in the water.

Once found, the men are hoisted aboard by the copter's small but powerful winch. The winchman might have to be lowered to help an injured man put the lifting strop around himself. The pilot has to take great care and flies to directions given by the winchman over an intercom: "six feet right, steady, down ten feet, steady." These directions ensure that the winch line does not get entangled with part of a wrecked ship or snag on the rock overhang on a cliff. At the same time the pilot has to watch that his rotors do not get damaged by flying too close to a dangerous cliff or electric supply cable and also that a sudden gust of wind does not push the plane against it. If the rotors get badly damaged the helicopter will crash.

As the rescue helicopter comes into land after winching the downed crew to safety, the pilot has to take care not to catch his rotors on the ship's aerials, its radar masts or other obstructions. An obvious precaution when flying any chopper, but with the rescue plane overloaded as it sometimes has to be with a rescued crew, he may not be able to hover as delicately as he would like and have to put down on the flight deck with more than a thump.

The search patterns may be varied when looking for a ship or ditched aircraft at sea, but they are charted to cover the area, as here in a series of squares. Their size will depend on the visibility, whether the sea is calm or rough, and the number of search aircraft available. But whatever the pattern, it is covered methodically by one or more aircraft.

12 Submarine and Mine Hunters

War at sea is now mainly a battle between submarines and the fleets which are trying to sink them. In this anti-submarine warfare (ASW), helicopters play a major part because they can lower a cylinder of sonar equipment into the sea, which may detect submarines far below the sur-face. This so(und) na(vigation) r(anging) kit sends out sound waves and measures the time these take to bounce back or "echo" from the seabed or any submerged object.

There may be five men in an ASW helicopter: the pilot, copilot, navigator, a winchman/gunner, and the sonar operator. Their work is co-ordinated as the chopper hovers and lowers the sonar to a depth of perhaps 330 feet (100m). Its echoes are fed up the wires of the winch to a display in the cabin which tells the experienced operator what is below the surface. Some types of sonar can be towed when in the water; others are dunked and then hoisted back inboard, after which the chopper flies to a new point in the search area to dunk the sonar again. Or it may be lowered to several different depths at each point. This speed of change in the sonar's position and the fact that it may be lowered some distance from friendly ships is the advantage of using this equipment from choppers. As when mounted in a ship that is

A Sea King crew withdraws its sonar after listening for submarines. The helicopter's radar scanners include one in the dome behind the engines on the fuselage top.

searching with others for the enemy, the ships' own hulls underwater may interfere with the sonar.

The ASW ships and aircraft are looking for a relatively small object in a great volume of ocean. But as submarines move through the water they and their engines make a noise that can be detected on acoustic sensors. Therefore the ASW fleets check areas of ocean for the sounds that are there naturally; then when a new sound is heard, this can be investigated.

The sound sensors may be in sonobuoys dropped from choppers. The buoy with its radio floats on the surface and automatically lowers its sensors to a preset depth. These can then pass back the noises they pick up and the chopper crew read these as radio signals. By dropping a pattern of buoys, the likely location and direction in which a submarine is moving may be worked out.

Helicopter crews may also use FLIR to detect the infrared waves from the warmer water of an atomic submarine's cooling system. Or they can use a Magnetic-Anomoly Detector (MAD), which shows where a submarine's steel hull is distorting the natural lines of magnetism in the search area, a useful means of checking if the sonar has picked up a steel hull or a whale.

Submarines can stay submerged for weeks but since radar does not work from under the water will raise their periscope radar from time to time in searching for ships to attack. This is a very small target indeed for the ASW fleet to spot. Yet chopper-borne radars like MEL's Super Searcher can see such a target even when there are large waves running which would cause a clutter of echos on other sets. This radar can also detect ships at a range of 135 miles (225km) if the chopper is flying high above the sea.

A second major threat from under the sea are mines. They may be set off in several different ways which make them dangerous to even mine hunting ships equipped to find them. Therefore a technique has been developed by which a helicopter tows a sledge, skimming over the water carrying mine detecting gear. If this sets off a mine, little damage will be done and the chopper crew flying high and ahead of the sled will not be caught in the explosion.

US Navy's MH-53E Sea Stallion tows a sledge to skim for mines.

13 Anti-Submarine Tactics

In the South Atlantic in the summer of 1982 squadrons operating their search patterns flew for hundreds of hours, but the only chance to attack a submarine fell to the Wessex HAS-3 of the destroyer HMS *Antrim* and the Wasp HAS-1s from the ice patrol ship HMS *Endurance*. Once the submarine had been found, the Wessex seriously damaged it with depth charges, and the two Wasps then attacked it with wire-guided missiles. The submarine could not submerge after these attacks but managed to reach harbor.

More powerful weapons can be used but the depth charges, dropped in a pattern near a submerged submarine, can cause it damage even though they do not fall and sink to explode right alongside the boat. Their high-explosive sends shock waves through the water which cause cracks in the sub's hull and can damage its machinery.

Even more dangerous for a submarine is the homing torpedo. This when launched from a chopper is guided close to the target by the sonar operator. He knows both the location of the sub and the track of the torpedo which shows up on his screen and guides it by signals passed along a wire similar to that which is used with TOW. Once he has the torpedo near his target and having satisfied himself that he is attacking an enemy submarine, he gives a final signal that sets the torpedo's sensors in operation. These are acoustic and track the noise of the submarine to home in on the target.

A chopper may drop Captor Mines which will lie in wait for the submarine expected to pass them. The mine casing sinks when dropped into the sea before releasing an anchor which holds it in position against tidal currents. The mine then floats some distance from the sea bed, the acoustic sensors of the torpedo it carries "listening" for the distinctive noise of an enemy submarine. When the

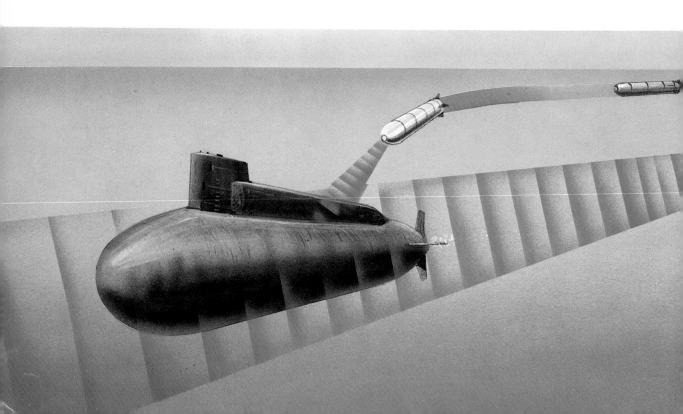

noises match the preset pitch and levels, the submarine's "signature," the mine releases the torpedo which tracks and hopefully hits the target.

It may be exploded, however, by decoys which are towed behind the submarine. These canisters are filled with electronic and other equipment which give out the noises expected from the submarine but do so with greater volume. The torpedo's sensors therefore track the decoys, explode on one of them and being far behind the submarine do it little or no damage.

The submarine captain can take other counter-measures against attack, releasing air bubbles which have the same effect on acoustic torpedoes as chaff has on radar: it confuses them. But the bubbles will rise to the surface, inviting a depth charge attack. Therefore the submariner probably tries to evade both torpedoes and depth charges by diving as deep as he can, to lie quietly with engines off and even no talking among the crew, in order not to be detected by listening devices.

Meanwhile the helicopters flying above the area work as part of a team with the surface ships, using sonar to find the submarine again, if their first attack failed. They may well have to go back to that search pattern which began the hunt, covering a wide area perhaps in quite a different part of the ocean to where they had made the unsuccessful attack. Because had the submarine escaped, it could well be 30 miles (50km) away from the scene in the forty minutes that the anti-submarine forces were trying to attack it.

The sonar operator in a helicopter (see below) uses the dunked sonar's echoes to guide an acoustic torpedo towards an enemy submarine. The torpedo when near its target then homes in using its own sensors.

14 Sea Reconnaissance and Actions Against Warships

Helicopters can find surface ships more easily than submarines, but if these are in a convoy they are likely to be escorted by aircraft. Therefore the tendency for shipborne helicopters is to shadow an enemy fleet using their radar. Such operations then become more a matter of electronic surveillance and counter-measures than a battle of bullets and missiles.

The Westland Lynx is equipped with sensors that warn the crew when the aircraft is in the scan of the enemy's radar, giving them time to fly clear. Yet as the Lynx can fly over 300 miles (500km) in a flight of three hours (its endurance), it may be far from its parent ship. In the subsequent battle to avoid being caught, the crew can use decoys and other deceptions to fox any missiles fired at them and have a warning system aboard which tells them if any enemy missile is locking onto the helicopter.

Although the Lynx can fly at 156 miles per hour (260km/h) or more in an emergency, such speed uses up fuel and therefore the crew have to dodge their enemies and keep enough fuel to reach their ship. This will be a tiny spec, in perhaps 600 square miles (1,000km²) of ocean, and a moving spec at that. Therefore the shipborne helicopter carries sophisticated navigation equipment, possibly including signals for satellites which are processed by the chopper's computer to give very precise readings of longitude and latitude, enabling a pilot to fly to a predetermined rendezvous with his ship.

When the frigate comes in range of an enemy ship, perhaps 18 miles (30km) away below the horizon, its Lynx may act not only as the ship's eyes, flying high enough to see the target, but also guide the ship's missiles to it. (This is necessary because radar waves are straight and do not follow the curve of the earth.) In such an action the helicopter may use its Ferranti Sea Spray Mark 3 Radar which can track several targets at one time passing information automatically by radio to a computer in the frigate, which then gives the ranges and other information necessary to aim the missiles at targets over the horizon. These having been launched, the chopper may guide them on the last part of their flight.

Shipborne choppers can also carry their own anti-ship missiles of which the Lynx has four Sea Skuas. These have a range of 9 to 12 miles (15-20km) depending on the chopper's height and speed at the time they are launched. Eight of these fired in rippled succession from two Lynx could

A Lynx helicopter's radar provides information on which its Frigate's missiles can be aimed at a target over the horizon from the view of the frigate's crew, its radar and other sensors. In all such maneuvers the Lynx flies only as high as is necessary to keep the enemy on its radar screen. Its pilot at times may be able to just pop up over-the-horizon and then below again. He can then see the target but he will be in view so briefly that enemy radar operators may not notice the Lynx.

A French Exocet AM-39 in flight skimming towards its target. The helicopter which launched this fire-and-forget missile has dropped below the horizon out of the view of the target ship.

sink a destroyer, yet this 319-pound (145-kg) missile is as easily loaded as the shell of a gun. On launching the guidance gyros are stabilizing the missile within 2 seconds as it flies at 0.80 Mach (four-fifths the speed of sound) skimming towards the target. Its course is programed to jink near the target in order to confuse enemy gunners but should it fail to hit the target, it blows up after 70 seconds of flight, ensuring it does not endanger friendly ships.

The most famous anti-ship missile, the Exocet, can also be fired from helicopters. It is three times heavier than the Sea Skua, has a range of 30 to 42 miles (50-70km) and can be guided to its target by several types of sensor as it is a fire-and-forget missile.

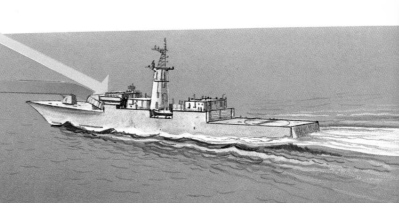

15 Commando Helicopters

Medium-sized helicopters like the British HC-4 Sea King and the American CH-46 Sea Knight can carry two dozen or more troops. The precise number depends on the weight of equipment each man carries, which can be 99 pounds (45kg) or more if he is carrying a couple of 81mm mortar shells or a radio. Such helicopters have been called "flying trucks" and are used widely by all military forces to carry men and combat stores in a battle area. Their ability to carry men ashore from ships of an amphibious force has fundamentally changed the techniques for seizing a beachhead.

Before the 1960s an amphibious assault was made in three stages. First paratroops or cliff-climbing commandos captured enemy coast guns. This ensured that ships could approach an enemy beach in reasonable safety. In stage 2 the assault companies landed to seize a beach. Then the main force came ashore in landing craft to consolidate the hold on the beachhead. But there were only relatively few beaches where landing craft might put men ashore. The defenders were therefore able to concentrate their forces at these points. But now they must be spread more thinly because choppers can cross a coast at many points, flying over cliffs, unaffected by offshore rocks which prevent landing craft reaching a beach.

Coast batteries will therefore now be seized by marine commandos landing near these guns, while others may be flown to landing zones (LZs) behind the beach defenses. There they can cut off the defenders from reinforcements, a technique using choppers that is known as vertical envelopment because it isolates the defenders.

The marines or soldiers in each chopper are known as a "stick," made up of riflemen, machine-gunners, signalers and others to suit the formation

The "stick" of troops loaded in a Sea King with their packs stowed by the door

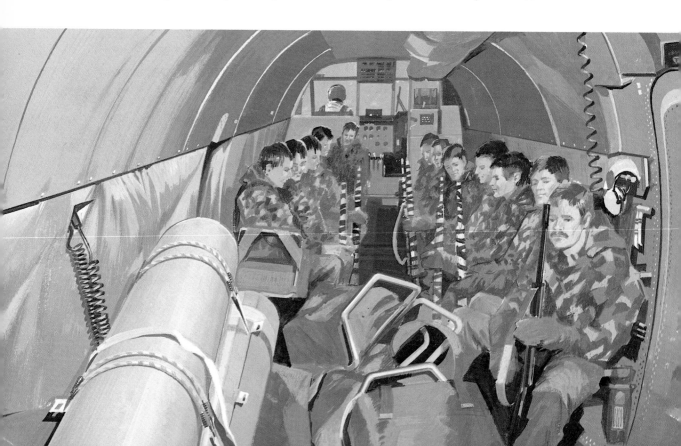

in which they will fight after landing. Each stick is loaded into a specific helicopter which will land near others carrying the remainder of the troop or platoon which will come into action immediately on landing.

As the helicopters take off in a steady stream to avoid accidents, and each must carry its correct stick, they must be loaded in a rehearsed sequence. The men being brought up from their quarters below decks arrive on the flight deck just before their chopper is ready to take off, a more difficult drill than it may sound for there may be 600 men to load into twenty helicopters. Should they get shot down or crash, each man has been trained to find the exit doors even if the plane is under water. He feels his way in this darkness, knowing by heart the shape of the cabin.

After the assault companies have landed, cleared the initial beachhead of enemy and made

Helicopters give logistic support here in carrying a Land Rover's trailer, a cargo net of ammunition boxes and an over-snow vehicle. Fifty such "lifts" are needed to move a Commando Battery of Royal Artillery with ammunition for its guns.

sure that the next flights of choppers cannot be attacked while hovering over their LZs, the main force are flown in. The choppers then return to their ships, circling them ready to land as ordered to collect combat supplies and fly these ashore.

Commando or transport helicopters may also be used at sea to transfer men and stores from one ship to another, cross-decking as it is called. Or they may be used to fly supplies to a ship in what is known as vertical replenishment. Such versatile uses of choppers at sea have made them indispensible to the navies of the world.

16 Combat Helicopters in Amphibious Warfare

The amphibious fleet will bombard a coast before the commando choppers fly in, the fire of these warships at times being controlled by a gunnery officer flying in a Lynx or an AH-64 to spot the fall of shells and redirect the gunners' aim. At other times he may have been landed secretly with a team of SAS or American Rangers the night before the bombardment. Choppers can insert such teams into enemy territory, undetected because they are mistaken for helicopters on reconnaissance. A Night Hawk HH-60D might make such a flight more easily than it can rescue crashed air crews.

There are obvious dangers in flying close to an area which is being shelled and therefore the bombardment stops before the commando choppers fly in to land troops. The trick is to time the arrival of combat choppers with their guns and rockets just as the bombardment lifts. The defenders then have no chance to reorganize because these choppers clear a path over the defenses. But should any ground radar still be operating, an EW chopper flies with the transport aircraft to jam this and missiles' sensors.

A US Marine Cobra attacks beach defenses as CH-53D Sea Stallions follow.

will have workshops and skilled technicians, who
As the landing develops, the combat choppers will attack any enemy strong points or tanks moving to support them. But the commander of the amphibious force knows that his helicopters need refueling and rearming, and cannot be airborne for more than an hour or two. During the early part of the battle they return to their ships to rearm, but as soon as there is a firm beachhead, a forward rearming point is set up ashore. Fuel is also taken ashore to this point, carried in large rubberized containers slung under helicopters.

About the same time, with the beachhead established, some of the carrier ships may put to sea, as they also carry ASW choppers. This can leave the landing force without adequate maintenance facilities for its choppers, and by the 1990s some navies plan to have helicopter support ships in their amphibious fleets. These converted merchantmen

can make major repairs that would not only be beyond the facilities of the small crew at a rearming point but even beyond the ground maintenance staff landed to provide a base for the helicopter squadrons.

For many years the commando ship was used with its choppers not only to land a force but also to supply it once ashore, a technique used extensively in Borneo by the British in the 1960s. At this time the commandos perfected the art of dropping to the treetops high over a tropical jungle as the chopper hovered in the difficult swirl of air currents over the jungle. Each man climbed down a rope from the chopper and carried 165 feet (50 m) of climbing rope. This he lowered from the high tree tops before climbing down to the jungle floor, a use for helicopters which was unthought of when the first flimsy military choppers flew in Burma during World War II.

17
Some Wartime Operations

Operation Musketeer

In the summer of 1956 the Egyptians took over the Suez Canal which was owned by the British and French governments who decided to send a force to make sure that the canal was kept open for the ships of all nations. It was spearheaded by 3 Commando Brigade RM which landed at Port Said in amphibious and assault craft, the airports to the east and west having been captured by British and French paratroopers the previous day.

In the first hours of this landing, 45 Commando were flown ashore by helicopters (see below). The first use of British choppers to land a sizeable force into a battle area. They were flown by 845 Squadron and others to land 55 minutes after the seaborne assault, a landing sequence dictated by

the experimental nature of the fourteen Whirlwinds and six small Sycamores in the role of troop carriers. These latter helicopters were not intended to carry troops and two of the three commandos in each aircraft sat with his legs dangling over the Sycamore's sides! Nevertheless 415 men and 23 tons of combat stores were landed, as the helicopters made several trips from two carriers. In all these took 83 minutes but was a faster time than would have been taken by landing craft having to make the 6.6 mile (11km) trip to carriers.

The operation showed the possibilities for the use of helicopters, and in the following years 845 became one of the most experienced commando helicopter squadrons. In the 1960s and '70s they landed commandos on many occasions during campaigns in Malaya, Borneo, Aden, and were most useful in the Falkland Island campaign of 1982.

Operation "Corporate"

In April 1982 after the Argentinians had invaded the Falkland Islands, eleven helicopter squadrons of the Royal Navy's Fleet Air Arm sailed with the Task Force to the South Atlantic. 845 had Wessex HU-5s at this time, 846 has Sea King HC-4s; the other squadrons had anti-submarine Sea Kings, Lynx and Wasps. Two of the HU-5s were lost in the gales and snow storms over South Georgia while trying to rescue special forces' teams. But they and the crashed crews were rescued by the brilliant flying of the pilot of a Wessex, who landed in these bleak mountains.

The remaining Commando choppers flew many missions to insert special forces' teams into the islands and none were detected by the Argentinian garrisons on East and West Falkland. The squadrons landed men of the SAS on Pebble Island for a major raid, and a few days later they put ashore part of the assault force that landed on East Falkland on the night of May 20 – 21. But none of the HC-4s carried weapons and therefore some had to be escorted by two Gazelles of the Command Brigade's Air Squadron, each of which carried a GPMG and 68mm rockets. They were shot down before they used these and sadly three of the four Marines flying in them were killed.

The remaining seven Gazelles and six Scout helicopters in this squadron flew urgently needed ammunition to the forward companies. They evacuated casualties, one pilot taking an injured man out of a mine field. They made recces and dodged enemy fighter-bombers. Although one Scout was shot down near Goose Green, a second pilot evaded an Argentinian Pucara by banking and turning this way and that to prevent his attacker getting a clear shot at the Scout.

Operation in Grenada

When the Americans were asked to assist the governments of several Caribbean states because the government of Grenada had been overthrown by a few desperate men, the aircraft carrier USS *Independence* and an amphibious force were sent to the Caribbean.

In the early hours of Tuesday October 25, 1983, US Seal Teams slipped ashore and recaptured the Governor's official residence. A few hours later on the northeast coast 400 Marines landed at Pearls airport in CH-46s from the assault ship USS *Guam*. They met little resistance but the 500 American Army Rangers parachuted to an airport to the south became involved in a battle as they advanced towards a college where 200 American students had been studying. These students were at some risk of being injured in the fighting until an American force landed by chopper on a nearby beach and lifted them to safety.

Two companies of Marines from Pearls were meanwhile taken back aboard *Guam*, to be landed in amphibians that evening at 7:30 PM on the west side of the island. These companies by early Wednesday morning were in the outskirts of St. George's, the capital of the island. They overran

A Marine AH-1T Cobra being refueled and rearmed aboard *Guam* off Grenada

several strong points as the five tanks with these Marines gave them covering fire. However isolated pockets of Grenadians continued to resist the Americans during the next few days, but with 5,000 American troops ashore by the Friday, the island was secured.

The use of Sea Knights in the initial landings had proved effective in getting the Marines ashore rapidly, although one CH-46 was lost when it came down in the sea near St George's. Two other helicopters were lost when Marine Cobra Squadrons were supporting both Army and Marine ground forces.

Men of 82 Airborne Division board UH-60As to fly to LZs in Grenadian mountains from which they mounted long-range patrols.

18   Gunships in 'Nam

When the former French colony of Indo-China became two separate republics, the North with Russian support began undermining the authority of the South's rulers. They in turn were helped by American military advisers, while for ten years secret agents from the North encouraged and supplied an "underground" army in the South. This Viet Cong force made terrorist attacks on the army of the South, using guerrilla tactics in quick strikes and major advances from their jungle bases. Therefore in 1965 United States Marines were landed to help defend the South's air bases. The enemy had many advantages of local help, jungle experience and almost fanatical determination. The Americans provided considerable technical resources for the South including a mastery in the air. Helicopters were able to fly therefore with virtually no interference except from ground anti-aircraft fire.

This air mastery led to the use of Air Cavalry, with its air-mobile skytroopers in Huey and Chinook helicopters. Typical of such units was the 11th Air Assault Battalion, its colonel and his tactical headquarters controlling ground operations from a command chopper.

Each company could be lifted by sixteen Hueys, eight of which would land at one time to pick up half a company, as they did on the morning of September 29, 1965, in the 11th Air Assault Battalion's first operation near An Khe in central Vietnam (see map). That morning the colonel and his tac HQ or Command Post flew for over an hour within sight of the target area about 1.8 miles (3km) from the American base at An Khe. The FAC directed strikes around the intended LZ; then the artillery bombarded it, the artillery's observer with the colonel directing this fire onto specific targets. This fire was stopped about two minutes before the rifle companies were due to land, but the enemy were given no chance to reorganize as four rocket-firing choppers blasted the intended landing zone for a minute. As they shifted their attacks to other targets, some of the gunships of an Assault Helicopter Battalion darted forward from protecting the Hueys approaching the LZ and fired their multiple cannons and heavy machine guns.

As the gunships flew away, the rifle companies' Hueys came in to land, the door gunners of the aircraft on the flanks spraying the area with machine gun fire. The first eight Hueys to land put down two platoons who fanned out quickly, setting up machine guns. Some shots were fired at the troops after they landed, but the enemy withdrew. Other platoons landed but 22 men were injured here or on patrols from this LZ by punji-sticks, the sharpened and hardened bamboo spikes which the enemy had hidden in the tall elephant grass. As patrols from B and C companies moved to search

A Huey UH-1B lands men of 7th Infantry Regiment to help the troops of these armored personnel carriers extract their vehicles from an enemy ambush.

up to 1,650 feet (500 m) of thick undergrowth around the LZ. They found a punji-stick"factory", some food stores and empty huts but none of the enemy. By 4:00 PM the colonel decided that his companies were not going to find any enemy guerrillas and the skytroopers were withdrawn.

Many such patrols were carried out in later months and years. The battalion also helped to pioneer several techniques including the transport of 105mm guns for underslung loads for Chinooks and the use of 132-foot (40-m) flexible ladders, by which they could climb from the jungle floor to a Chinook hovering above the jungle treetops.

The vast areas these mobile troops could cover is exemplified by 1 Air Cavalry Division which in December 1965 operated over an area stretching from the coast to the Cambodian border and 114 miles (190km) north and a similar distance south of

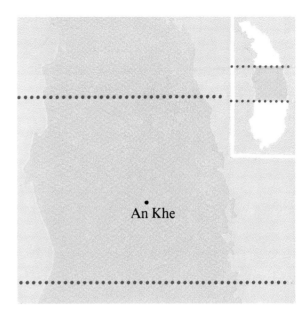

South Vietnam in the 1960s showing the area covered by 1 Air Cavalry Division in the winter of 1965-6

An Khe. An area half the size of Scotland or of Indiana. They set up some LZs which were permanently defended; others they used after these had been recced from the air. They carried out rescue missions, landing their troops to help armored and other patrols ambushed on highways, sometimes being heavily attacked along a mile of road before the enemy dispersed back into the jungle.

A Chinook CH-47 makes the recovery of an APC from water-logged rice fields look easy.

19
Heavy Lifts

The war in Vietnam had shown not only the value of utility and gunship helicopters but also the need for larger helicopters to lift forty or more men in one aircraft. Ivan Sikorsky saw how this might be done by redesigning his sky crane, the S-60 which first flew in 1958, see below. It could lift a section of bridge or other building work to places which could not be reached by road. The new design of aircraft became the Sea Stallion with a large cabin and twin engines of 3,500hp, and by the mid-1960s was being used to fly US Marines.

The advantage of large choppers is that they can be loaded with small vehicles driven up a ramp at the rear of the cabin. This could provide 140 cubic feet (40m^3) of space for stowing supplies or the vehicle taken aboard might itself be loaded with combat supplies. In 1968 Sea Stallions were carrying loads of 28,000 pounds (12,700kg) and when unloaded could virtually loop the loop despite their size. They could also carry the heavy radar and radio equipment of those days with an automatic pilot to fly the plane at a constant distance above the ground, rising and falling as it crossed hills into valleys. They became known affectionately as the "Jolly Green Giants" because of their dark green camouflage. USMC choppers are still this color, but some naval AS choppers have a blue and grey color scheme to make them more difficult to see against the sky.

Another heavy lift helicopter that came into service in 1962 was the American Boeing Vertol Company's Chinook, with its twin rotors each 59.4 feet (18m) in diameter. These, like most heavy choppers, are not expected to fly over enemy defenses, although four were armed in 1965 with machine guns, grenade launchers and quick-firing cannons, including a gunner's position on the rear ramp, weaponry which led them to be called "Go-Go-Birds."

The largest helicopters were built in Russia in 1985, as these are needed in Siberia where the snow

Below: S-60 helicopter crane

Left: A CH-53E Super Stallion, in some respects a descendant of the S-60 but with three engines, lifts a section of bridge. It can also carry 45 men from an assault company or lift 1.45 ton, be refueled in flight from tankers or when hovering over a ship. It is also used by the US Navy to resupply ships at sea in vertical replenishment and by naval construction battalions building fleet forward bases.

and ice make the upkeep of surfaced roads very expensive. Their Mi-26 *Halo* can carry 44,000 pounds (20,000kg) for 480 miles (800km), lifted by its 8-bladed rotor, 106 feet (32m) in diameter. Heavy loads can be put aboard from trucks using the plane's own lifting tackle and hydraulic ramp. Stowing such loads is therefore easy but they must be well secured, a job the pilot can check without leaving his seat as he has a TV screen on which he can select any of three different views of the great cargo-hold to make sure it is correctly loaded. All chopper pilots are responsible for loads being unable to shift should the plane run into air turbulence. Although the *Halo* is flown in the Russian civilian air services, almost all choppers in the USSR have military uses in wartime.

The Americans are building an even larger Boeing experimental (X) CH-62. This will be able to lift 69,850 pounds (31,750kg) and therefore can carry an M110 Self-Propelled gun as an underslung load.

Above: The Giant Russian Mi-26 *Halo* here in the livery of the civilian airline Aeroflot can lift 20 ton (20,000kg).

Below: The CH-47 Chinook which is 99 feet (30m) long when the rotors are turning, is dwarfed by a mock-up of the XCH-62 that is designed to lift 31.75 ton and expected to be flying with the US forces later in the 1980s.

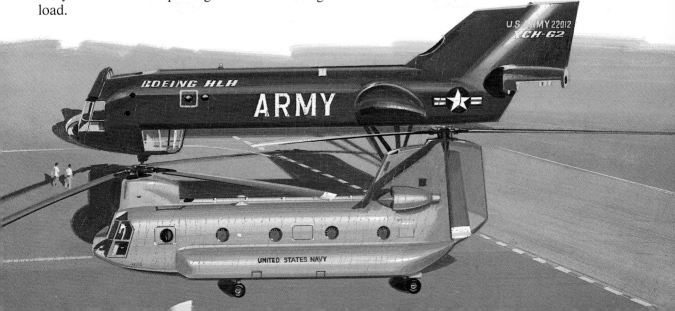

20
The Future

Work in the mid-1980s on new designs of aircraft which can take off vertically cover not only larger choppers but some other forms of aircraft. These make use of new materials and engines, including new systems of controlling the aircraft's tail and rotor pitch. The new materials have led to the composite airframe which has far fewer parts. It is therefore easier to assemble and maintain during operations.

New designs of engine are being built in several cases by countries joining together to share the high cost, as have France and Germany in building a new engine for the PAH-2. One new system replaces the mechanical wires, levers and rods which work the plane's hydraulic pumps used in moving, say, a tail plane. Instead of wires, a fiber-optic cable carries light signals to switch on and off these pumps or reverse them. The signals being sent automatically as the pilot moves his control column.

New designs of conventional helicopters for the 1990s include the EH 101 (see illustration) being built by Augusta of Italy and Westland. It will fly for 5 hours without refueling and cover 600 miles (1,000km), carrying new types of electronics in its ASW role and electronic jamming devices. It will be armed with missiles that may be fired either at tanks or other aircraft, a mast-mounted sight and sensors.

The shape of helicopters in the 1990s is likely to be slimmer in order to make them harder to detect on radar. They may have the Advancing Blade (AB) type of twin rotors with stiff blades. As these rotate they are advancing ahead of the aircraft's speed of flight, and when this is fast flight they provide most of the lift. They are likely to be 90 miles per hour (150km/h) faster than equivalent helicopters with variable-pitch rotors. They can also fly in the thin air above 1.8 miles (3km), which is the maximum height for most helicopters at the present. They do not need a tail rotor, see right illustration, and their forward thrust may therefore come from a shrouded pusher propeller.

The combination of sensors, navigation aids and the aircraft's computer, its avionics, will enable one man not only to fly it but also fire its weapons, use its jamming devices and decoy air missiles away from the plane. Its weapons will be housed under covers in the fuselage until they are required, as will its landing gear retracting as this does on fixed-wing aircraft. The weapons may be aimed by use of helmet-mounted displays, "pictures" in light projected onto the pilot's visor, enabling him to see through this grid of lines as if looking along a rifle sight. He may give the order to fire by speaking to his computer in the way that he can give it other directions by voice.

The EH 101 is being built in co-operation by a British and an Italian company for military service in the 1990s.

All this is a far cry from the noisy, uncomfortable and sometimes unreliable helicopters of two generations ago, and in the next generation they will be simple to handle and less easily distinguished from their close relative, the tilt-rotor aircraft. (The tilt-rotor planes use their 23-foot (7-m) propellers in a horizontal position to lift them vertically off the ground or to hover).

As for changes in tactics, these aircraft with their advanced avionics will enable squadrons to not only monitor a battle, reporting events to headquarters, to attack armor and aircraft, but also to carry out these roles over a large area of several hundred miles in depth and width. Then as ground forces are dispersed against possible nuclear attack, the scene of a battle may extend thousands rather than hundreds of miles across the countryside, with the helicopters, the tanks, the troops in Light Armored Vehicles (LAVs) all moving to coordinated attacks that have been programed by computers. Such battles may last 90 minutes rather than a day before one or the other side is forced to withdraw; in this final stage helicopters will dominate the action, the victor's machines harrassing the vanquished while his helicopters cover the ground troops' withdrawal.

Below: Bell Helicopter Textron's Light helicopter Experimental (LHX) with tilt rotors, single seater cockpit and a dash speed of 198 mph (330 km/h)

Above: An impression of the Advancing Blade Concept (ABC) helicopter with its twin stiff bladed rotors and pusher propeller in the tail

Abbreviations

ABC	Advancing Blade Concept
ADMS	Air Defense Suppression Missile
AFCS	Automatic Flight Control System
AH	Attack or Anti-tank Helicopter
AH-1T+	Cobra Attack Helicopter type 1T plus equipment for USMC operations
AMS	Avionic Management System
AS	Anti-Submarine
ASW	Anti-Submarine Warfare
CG	Chain Gun
CH	Combat Helicopter (American)
CH	Commando Helicopter (British)
DZ	Dropping Zone
FAA	Fleet Air Arm
FAC	Forward Air Controller
FLIR	Forward Looking Infrared
GPMG	General Purpose Machinegun
HAS	Helicopter Anti-Submarine
HH	Heavy Helicopter (weighing 10 ton or more)
hp	Horsepower
HU	Helicopter Utility (obsolete)
IR	Infrared
LAV	Light Armored Vehicle
LZ	Landing Zone
MAD	Magnetic-Anomaly Detector
NOE	Nap Of Earth
OH	Observation Helicopter
OTH	Over The Horizon
PAH	*Panzerabwehr-Hubschauker*
PNG	Passive Night Goggles
RAF	Royal Air Force
RM	Royal Marines
SAR	Search And Rescue
SAS	Special Air Service
Seal	Sea Air Landing (Team)
SEMA	Special Electronic Mission Aircraft
SONAR	Sound Navigation Ranging
SOTAS	Standoff Target Acquisition System
TH	Training Helicopter
VDU	Visual Display Unit
UH	Utility Helicopter
USMC	United States Marine Corps
WRNS	Women's Royal Naval Service

Glossary

ADVANCING BLADE CONCEPT
Use of stiff rotors to give lift at high speed

AUTOMATIC PILOT
This AFCS system keeps the aircraft on a preset course.

AVIONICS
The use in aircraft of the technology of electronics

"BIRD"
American army slang for helicopter

"CHOPPER"
Slang for helicopter.

COMPOSITE AIRFRAME
Body of aircraft built mainly of panels not unlike those of motorcars

DASH SPEED
Short burst of high-speed that uses fuel quickly

ELECTRONIC COUNTERMEASURES
Jamming of radar and other surveillance equipment by means of electronic waves

HELMET DISPLAY
Optical projection of gun sight or instrument readings onto the pilot's helmet visor.

HOT REFUELING
Taking on fuel with engines running

INFRARED
"Black light" which cannot be seen because its wavelength is longer than light waves

LASER BEAM
Narrow beam of light with only one wavelength

RADAR SCAN
The sweep of a radar beam as the transmitting aerial rotates

PASSIVE EQUIPMENT
Devices which operate without sending out a beam, as in passive night goggles which enable their wearer to see at night without projecting a flashlight-type beam

SKY TROOPER
An enlisted man (private) in the US Air Cavalry

STAND-OFF TARGET
One that can be seen from a distance beyond the range of its weapons

VERTICAL ENVELOPMENT
The surrounding of defences by assault troops landed from helicopters

VERTICAL REPLENISHMENT
Resupply of ships be helicopter

WEAPONS SYSTEM
The combination of cannon, rockets, bombs or other weapons carried by an aircraft or a ship

Index